This Book Belongs To

_____

_____

_____

Bonus

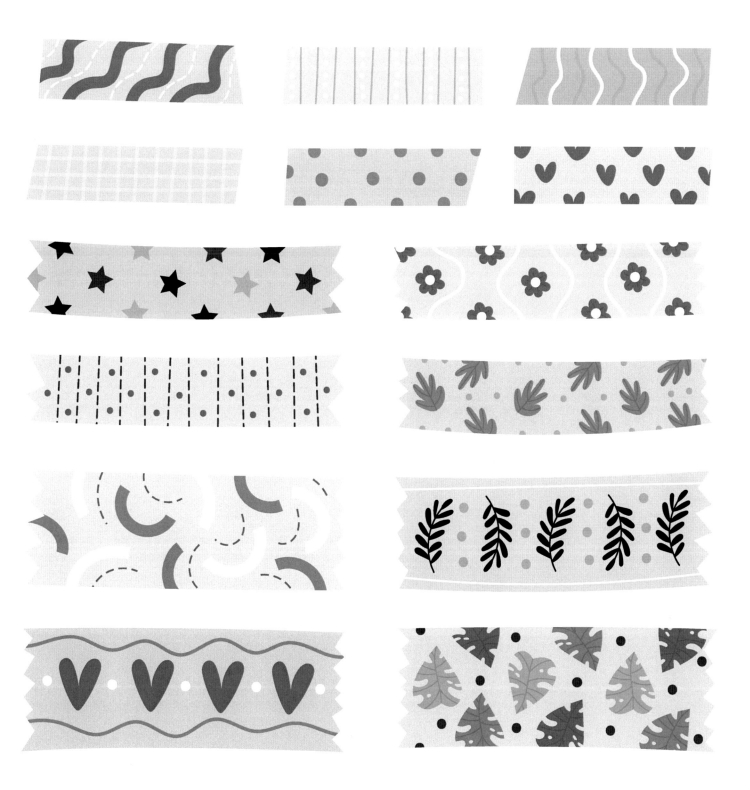

Fitness
Self-care
Mindfulness
Self-love
Career
Dream Home
Alphabets
Motivational Words
Inspirational Quotes
Boarding Pass
Pets
Travel
Family & Friends
Wedding

Examples

Fitness

STRENGTH

HEALTH

Discipline

WORKOUT

WORKOUT

Exercise

SELF
♡
CARE

MIND
BODY
+ SOUL
_____
YOU

Self-Care

Loveliness

SELF CARE
IS
THE NEW
HEALTH
CARE

WORKING:
ON MYSELF
BY MYSELF
FOR MYSELF

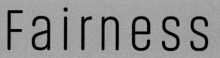

Fairness

Self Care Package

You deserve to be kind to yourself

For You

Glamor

Mindfulness

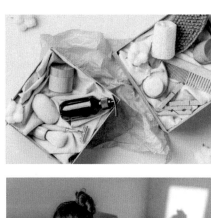

SELF CARE

ISN'T

SELFISH

BUILD
SELF CARE
HABITS AND
RITUALS

Self Care

SELF CARE DOESN'T
ALWAYS MEAN
THE SAME THING

Self Love

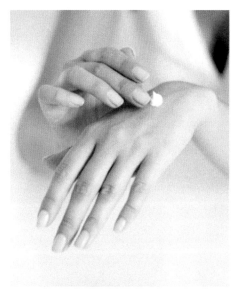

Sleep

Well Being

NEXT EXIT ↗

Care Free

Attention

Grace

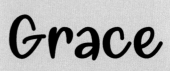

Elegance

Cute

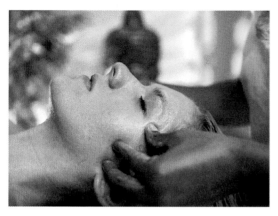

GLOW

HOME SWEET HOME

you are my home

MY DREAM HOME

Study Room

Dream Kitchen

I AM BEAUTIFUL	I AM BRAVE	I AM SMART
I AM KIND	I AM PASSIONATE	I AM LOVED
I AM ENOUGH	I AM LOUD	I AM WANTED

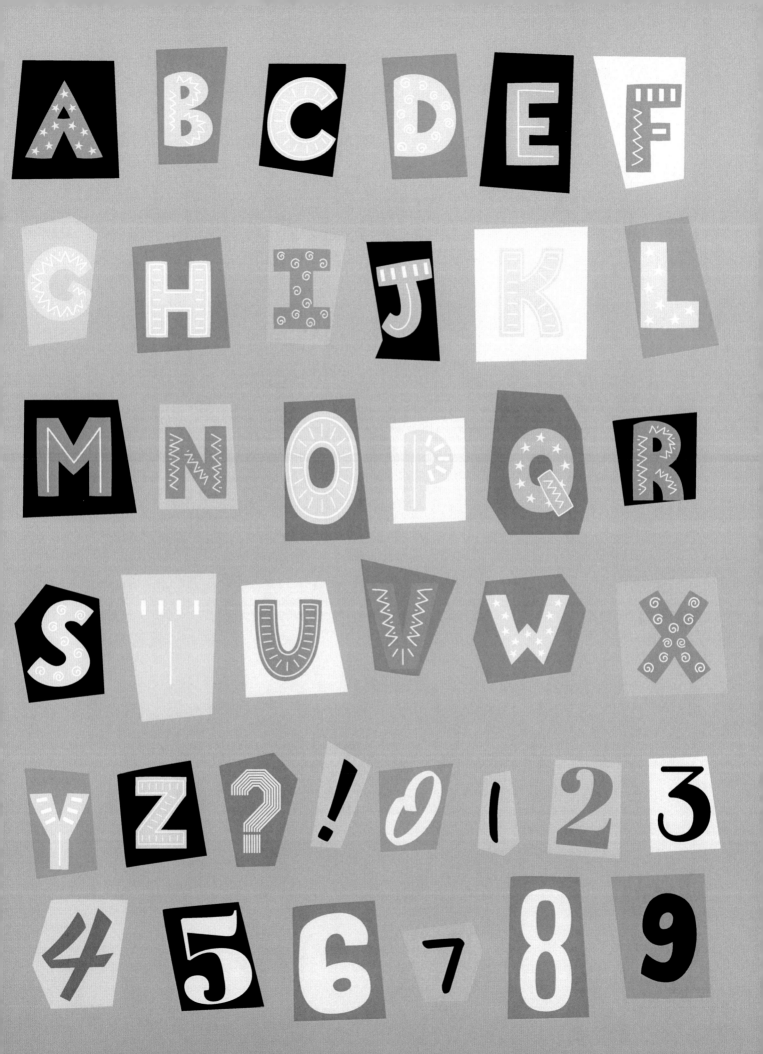

FUN!

Travel

Savings

BABY

Friendship

Adventure

Wedding

Enjoy

SUCCESS

MINDFULNESS

NEW HOME

NEW CAR

Spirituality

LIVING HOME

FAMILY

FITNESS

Skin Care

NEW ME

WIN

TIME

SLAY

Confident

Friends

healthy

Beautiful

MANIFESTATION BANK

No. 1234567

DATE ☐ ☐ ☐ ☐ ☐ ☐ ☐
D D M M Y Y Y

Pay To _____

The Sum of US Dollar _____ US $ _____

_____

_____
Authorized Signature

MANIFESTATION BANK

No. 1234567

DATE ☐ ☐ ☐ ☐ ☐ ☐ ☐
D D M M Y Y Y

Pay To _____

The Sum of US Dollar _____ US $ _____

_____

_____
Authorized Signature

MANIFESTATION BANK

No. 1234567

DATE ☐ ☐ ☐ ☐ ☐ ☐ ☐
D D M M Y Y Y

Pay To _____

The Sum of US Dollar _____ US $ _____

_____

_____
Authorized Signature

BOARDiNG PASS 18A

FIRST CLASS TICKET – AIR LINES

NAME OF PASSENGER

BOOIG00

DESTINATION

89B – NYC

DATE

22/09/18

BOARDiNG PASS 18A

FIRST CLASS TICKET – AIR LINES

NAME OF PASSENGER

BOOIG00

DESTINATION

89B – NYC

DATE

22/09/18

BOARDiNG PASS 18A

FIRST CLASS TICKET – AIR LINES

NAME OF PASSENGER

BOOIG00

DESTINATION

89B – NYC

DATE

22/09/18

Statue of Liberty	Paris
Dubai	Bali
New York	Athens
Bangkok	Colosseum
Tajmahal	Egypt
Maldives	Amsterdam
Rome	Cape Town
Niagra Falls	England
Great Wall of China	Statue of Liberty

PAINTING	GARDENING
COOCKING	PHOTOGRAPHY
WRITING	SPORTS
HIKING	CALLIGRAPHY
COACHING	DANCING
READING	GAMING
DRAWING	ARCHERY
BLOGING	YOGA
SINGER	CYCLING

If you **Believe** IN YOURSELF *Anything* IS POSSIBLE

You ARE THE **ARTIST** *of your own* LIFE

the **BEST** *is yet* TO BE

Self *love is your* **SUPER** *power*

You ONLY *Regret* *What* *you* *Don't Do*

BE GOOD TO *yourself*

Alone but not *Lonely*

THE *Best* *is* *Yet* *to* **COME**

We are ALL *in this* TOGETHER

You *Can* **DO** *it*

Work *Sweat* *achieve*

DRINK *more* WATER

We BECOME What We THINK ABOUT

Work HARD Dream BIG

Be STRONG

SMILE are always in FASHION

THE WAY YOU SPEAK YOUR-SELF matters

one day at a time

GREAT Thing TAKE TIME

STAY strong

time for a break

START BEFORE YOU'RE READY

DON'T BE SO HARD ON Yourself

BREAK THE Stigma

Pets

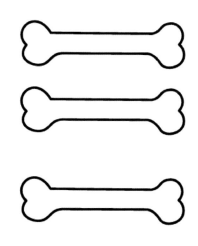

NEVER LEAVE
your Dog BEHIND

I Love Pet's

Work
HARD
Dream
BIG

my dog is my
BFF♡

Travel & Adventure

TRAVEL

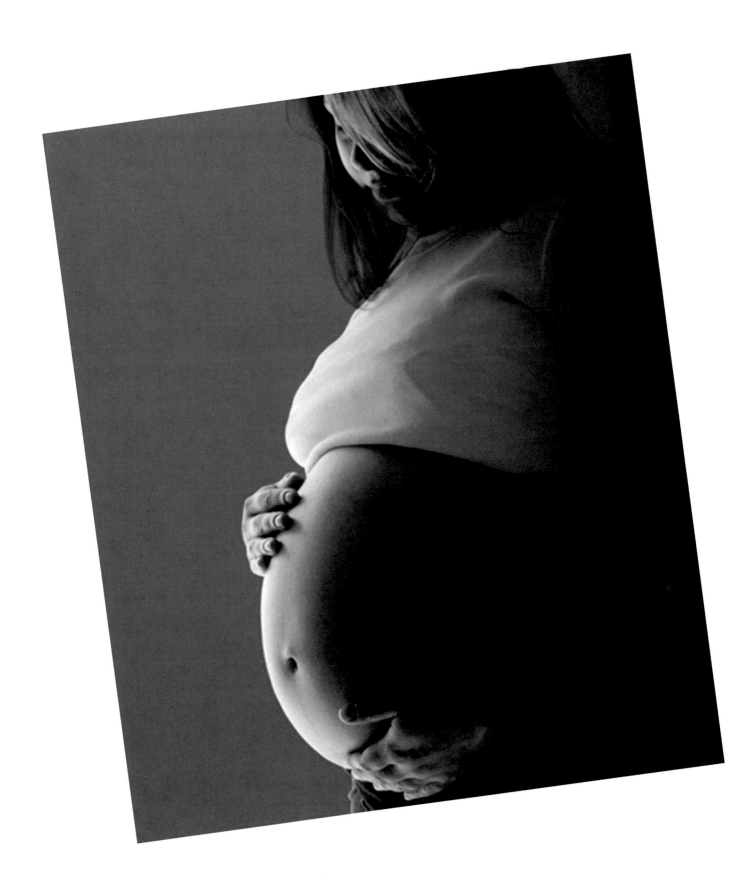

Adventure time

EXPLORE more

ADVENTURE

family

memories

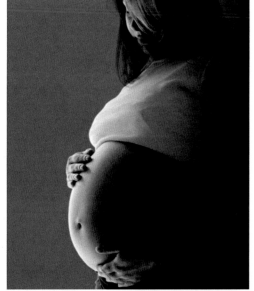

My Family

We are
~ALL~
in this
TOGETHER

friends

will you marry me?

bestie

Magic is
in you

Magic
moments

sweet
moments

BIG
Sister

LOVE

Thank you!!

— o o o —

From Lily Bee Publishing, where every splash of creativity brings mindfulness stress-relief and relaxation!

Founded by a dynamic mother-daughter duo, we specialize in creating vibrant books to bring joy to all.

Thank you for choosing our book,. We apreciate your feedback and would love if you could please leave us an honest review ♥

— o o o —

Share with Us!!

○ ○ ○

We would love to see your works of art. You can share them on our FaceBook page here.

SCAN ME

Made in United States
Orlando, FL
15 December 2024